# The Sisters of Thistle

a screenplay by
Christina Hamlett

Editorial Note:

The font and format of this script do not adhere to the rules of industry standard and, accordingly, should not be used as a template for anyone who gets inspired to go pen his or her own screenplay. These elements have been purposely modified to facilitate the story's reading ease for those among you who don't read screenplays for a living.

# ACKNOWLEDGMENTS

This turn-of-the-century work of fiction is a nod to two of my favorite places in the world—Scotland (where my beloved and I exchanged our wedding vows) and Alexandria, Virginia (where I'm pretty sure I must have lived in a prior lifetime).

# The Sisters of Thistle

FADE IN:

EXT. THISTLEBURN ABBEY - RAINY
MORNING

TITLE CARD: THISTLEBURN ABBEY,
SCOTLAND, 1881

*Traveling shot toward a stone abbey of modest size in the
Scottish countryside. A carriage waits just outside of it.*

MICHAEL (V.O.)
Hush y' now, lass.  It won't be so bad.

IAN (V.O.)
N' didna y' hear 'im promise to
write every day 'n' twice on
Sunday?  There be somethin'
to hang your hat on!

INT. THISTLEBURN ABBEY

*MICHAEL MCKAY (20's) and his best friend IAN
SUTHERLAND (20's) are young Scotsmen dressed for travel and
bidding goodbye to Michael's little sister (unseen) in a wingback chair.
Michael kneels in front of it as Ian and the humorless SISTER
HONORE (50's) look on.*

SISTER HONORE
Need I be remindin' y', Mr.
Sutherland that the Sabbath is
the Lord's day set aside for
devotionals.

IAN
Well y'd not be findin' a
brother more devoted than
himself here, would y' now,
Sister?

MICHAEL
I love y' with all my heart, Fiona.
Y' not be forgettin' that now?

*FIONA (5) is a very pretty but very sad little girl. She shakes her head gravely. Michael brushes away her tears.*

MICHAEL (CONT'D)
And y' promise to do as the
good sisters tell y' til I be
sendin' passage to join Ian 'n'
myself?

IAN
Y' not be sendin' passage at all
if we miss the bloody boat.

*Sister Honore clears her throat in disapproval of his language.*

IAN (CONT'D)
Say your goodbyes, Michael.
They'll not be waitin' for us.

*Fiona grabs Michael's sleeve.*

MICHAEL
Sure as it tears me apart, lass,
but we talked it all through.
Show us a brave face like y'
practiced.

*Her smile is brave but forced.*

4

SISTER HONORE
You'd not be expectin' a bairn to
understand the impossible, Mr. McKay.

MICHAEL
Aye, but there y' be wrong,
Sister. Nothin' is impossible
in America. Not e'en for the
likes of us. Come on now,
Fiona. See me to the door 'n'
I'll blow a big kiss for y' to
catch and put 'neath your
pillow.

*She brightens a little at this and climbs off the chair. He takes her
hand as Ian gets their bags. Sister Honore follows them to the door,
her opinion of their plans undisguised.*

INT/EXT.

*Ian proceeds to the carriage. Michael lingers a moment.*

MICHAEL
(to Sister Honore)
I'll be sendin' the money
regular when Ian 'n' me get on
our feet.

SISTER HONORE
See that y' do.

MICHAEL
Do the best y' can, Sister Honore. I'd
not be wantin' her to go without.

SISTER HONORE
Tis the Lord's choice, Mr.
McKay. Not mine.

IAN
Michael!

MICHAEL
(to Fiona)
I'll be back before y' know it.

*He starts toward the carriage, turns and blows Fiona the promised kiss. She jumps up to catch it with both hands, happily grinning as he beams his approval.*

*As the carriage starts to leave, Sister Honore and Fiona are joined in the doorway by the pinch-faced SISTER BRIDGET (50's). She, too, watches the departure with some discomfiture.*

SISTER BRIDGET
America, is it?  Such a faraway
place to go!

SISTER HONORE
Too far.

SISTER BRIDGET
Will they be comin' back, do y' think?

*The pair are seemingly oblivious that their new ward has ears and is listening to every word.*

SISTER HONORE
Their kind *never* come back, Sister
Bridget.  Not from America, they don't.

SISTER BRIDGET
No?

SISTER HONORE
Too much temptation.

SISTER BRIDGET
Virginia did I hear 'im say?

SISTER HONORE
Aye.

SISTER BRIDGET
Sure as a place named for our
blessed Virgin Mother has to
have a *bit* o' good in it.

SISTER HONORE
Far from it 'n' then some.  Far
from it indeed.

*A bewildered Fiona intently watches the carriage become*
*smaller, even as Sister Bridget firmly takes her hand to pull her*
*inside.*

SISTER BRIDGET
Come along with y', wee
Fiona.  You'll be catchin' your
death.

*Sister Honore firmly closes the door on the outside world.*

DISSOLVE TO:


EXT. ABBEY DOOR - MORNING

TITLE CARD: 16 YEARS LATER.

*CU of male hand knocking on a door which is much weathered*
*from the last time we saw it.  It is opened by a sweet tempered*
*and beautiful young nun whom we will come to realize is the*
*grown-up version of FIONA.  She brightens when she sees the*
*caller is SEAMUS, the local letter carrier, but is puzzled as*
*to why he's out of breath.*

FIONA
Sure as the day just started,
Seamus, 'n' look at yourself--
already outa breath!

*He thrusts a letter into her hands.*

SEAMUS
I ran all the way when I seen
who it come from. I thought
y'd be wantin' it.

*She smiles, sliding her fingertips over its surface.*

SEAMUS (CONT'D)
Doin' well for 'imself o'er
there, is he?

FIONA
Aye. Just as he promised.

SEAMUS
So will y' be leavin' us, Sister?

FIONA
'N for what reason would *that*
be?

SEAMUS
Didna y' always say y'd be
going there, too?

FIONA
A long time ago, Seamus. I
can't imagine he'd be wantin'
me to come now...

INT. FIONA'S ROOM - MOMENTS LATER

*She sits on her narrow cot reading Michael's letter. A stack of his earlier letters, tied up with a string, sits on the bed beside her.*

FIONA (V.O.)
Dearest Fiona. Y'd best be
sittin' down for the news, I
think, 'n' quite a bit o' it as
well. Ian has taken himself a
bride at last 'n' none too soon
I tease him. She's a fine lass
named Catherine 'n' tolerant,
too, if y'd be recalling his
fondness for the spirits. The
crops have done well by us--

MICHAEL (V.O.)
(taking over reading)
--better than we thought for
the wretched rains last winter.

DISSOLVE TO:

INT. MICHAEL'S STUDY, ALEXANDRIA
VIRGINIA

*He is sitting at a desk in what looks to be a cozy corner of a small room and writing a letter. The camera gradually pulls out to reveal it is not only a large room but is also part of a well-appointed mansion.*

MICHAEL (V.O.)
There be a demand we can barely
keep up with... '...n' sure as it's to
your bedside prayers we can be
thankful for its continuance. Which
brings me to why I be writin' with a
sense of urgent. Y' need to bid your

goodbyes to the Sisters of Thistle,
Fiona, 'n' come join me in the state
of Virginia. Tis a promise I made
before Mum 'n' Da passed that y'd
never be wantin' sure as I had the
wits 'n' the coin to provide for us.

*He pauses and gazes fondly out the upper story window on an
expansive tobacco planation. He picks up the letter.*

*POV Michael: Letter text.*

MICHAEL (V.O.)
You'll not be disagreein' when
y' see it at last that I've finally
done all right enough to send
y' proper passage.

MATCH CUT TO:

INT. THISTLEBURN ABBEY - LATER

*SFX: A raspy female cough*

*The letter is in the hands of Sister Honore, now Mother
Superior of the small order. The years have not been kind to
her looks nor her health. She shoots Fiona a stern look.*

SISTER HONORE
Pride goeth before the fall,
Sister Fiona.

FIONA
Aye, Mother Superior.

SISTER HONORE
Your brother Michael--he boasts of
himself like a fancy millionaire.

FIONA
He 'n' Ian worked hard for
themselves to be sure.  And
doesn't the Good Book say--

SISTER HONORE
Tis frivolous 'n' that's that.  Y'd
best be returnin' his ill got gains 'n'
think nothin' more of it.

FIONA
But I miss him so, Mother
Superior.  'N' it'd only be for a
short time, I think.

SISTER HONORE
A short time, she says!  Have
you forgotten he used the
same words when he took
leave of us?

FIONA
I'll be back before y' know it.  He
said those words as well.  Same as
y' be hearin' 'em from me.

SISTER HONORE
E'en if I were to say yes--'n'
I'm not sayin' I would--y'd not
be safe twixt here 'n' there.

FIONA
Not e'en with the Lord's
protection?

SFX: Rap on the open door.

Sister Honore looks up to see Sister Bridget.

11

SISTER BRIDGET
Sorry to be interruptin'--

*She casts an anxious glance at Fiona, then Sister Honore.*

SISTER HONORE
Yes?

SISTER BRIDGET
(bites her lip)
She's doin' it again.

SISTER HONORE
Again?

*She looks at Fiona. Fiona offers a helpless shrug.*

FIONA
I told her the sound was
displeasin' but--

SISTER HONORE
But what, Sister Fiona? Twas
your responsibility to see that she
follows the rules of the order if
she's to have sanctuary here.

FIONA
Aye, but seein' as how she's
not one of us--

*Sister Honore shoots her a withering glare. Fiona scoots back
her chair to go attend to the unspoken problem.*

FIONA (CONT'D)
I'll be speakin' to her about it.

SISTER HONORE
See that y' do.

FIONA
'N' about the letter...?

SISTER HONORE
Y' need to be searchin' your
*own* heart on that one.  Tis the
Lord's choice to give y'
answer.

*Fiona nods and exits.  Sister Bridget waits until she has left to
approach the desk and point to the letter still in the Mother
Superior's hands.*

SISTER BRIDGET
The brother again, is it?

*Sister Honore hands it to her.*

SISTER HONORE
Promises he makes her...'n'
money for a ship's voyage as
well!

SISTER BRIDGET
Sure as y'd not be holdin' her
from the journey then?

SISTER HONORE
There be nothin' in his grand land
of Virginia she couldn't find here.

SISTER BRIDGET
Except perhaps her own kind.

*Sister Honore gives her the same stern look.*

SISTER BRIDGET
Beggin' to differ with y', of course.

SISTER HONORE
Her own kind is *here*, Sister
Bridget. Not even a journey
of a thousand miles can
change it.

SISTER BRIDGET
Only a thousand, is it? I'd have
thought Virginia was much farther...

*SFX: A female voice cheerfully sings A BIRD IN A GILDED
CAGE.*


INT. ABBEY DINING HALL - CONTINUOUS

*POV Fiona as she approaches from behind the figure who is
feather-dusting the backs of the chairs. It is DAPHNE
HEDGES, a striking blond Englishwoman (late 20's) whose
confidence and physique would seem better suited to a dance hall
than a convent. She wears a long skirt and Victorian blouse.
Fiona clears her throat to get the young woman's attention.*

DAPHNE
Fiona! You're just in time for
the chorus!

*She starts to open her mouth to resume the song but Fiona
quickly puts her hand up in a "Shhh" gesture. Puzzled,
Daphne playfully mimics it.*

DAPHNE (CONT'D)
Shhhh?

*Fiona approaches her, dropping her voice to a whisper.*

FIONA
It's Sister Bridget.  She told
Mother Superior y'd been
singin' bawdy songs again.

DAPHNE
Oh bother!  Why doesn't she just count
her rosaries and leave me alone?

FIONA
Sure as I don't mind your
songs myself--'n' some o' the
others as well, I think--but--

DAPHNE
How can you live with so
many rules?  If I stay here
forever, I swear I'll never
understand it.

*She notices Fiona's pained expression.*

DAPHNE (CONT'D)
Sorry.  I'm not supposed to
say "swear" either, am I?

FIONA
It's not just that, I'm afraid.

DAPHNE
There's more?

*It's clear Fiona hates to be the bearer of bad news.  She pulls
out a chair to sit down, takes a deep breath, and delivers her
message.*

FIONA
When first y' came here,
Daphne, we couldn't turn y'
away.

*Daphne pulls out a chair, too.*

DAPHNE
I should hope not!  It was
bloody raining cats and dogs!

FIONA
If y'd be recallin' then, it was three
months ago this comin' Saturday.

*Daphne leans back and puts her feet on the table, revealing fashionable, high-laced boots.*

DAPHNE
Has it been that long already?

FIONA
Accordin' to Mother
Superior...
(she hesitates)
...it's been a wee bit *too* long.

DAPHNE
Meaning what?

*Fiona leans forward to take Daphne's hand.*

FIONA
Y' be my dearest 'n' best friend
since y' came... 'n' high praise
it is, too, you're not bein' a
Sister o' Thistle yourself.

DAPHNE
God, I should hope not.
(beat)
Sorry.  As you were saying...?

FIONA
They'd be wantin' y' to make a choice.
In order to stay on that is.

DAPHNE
What kind of choice, exactly,
are we talking about?

FIONA
(with difficulty)
Y' either need to be takin' the veil and
doin' the Lord's good work--

DAPHNE
What's the *other* choice?

FIONA
The other choice...is to go
back to the family y' came
from.

*Daphne explodes out of the chair, much to Fiona's concern.*

DAPHNE
Bloody hell not!

FIONA
But sure as they must be
wonderin' where y' be!

DAPHNE
I'd sooner hop a ship to--to *America*
than ever see *their* likes again!

INT. CHAPEL - EVENING

*CU of candles burning*

FIONA (O.C.)
Can y' not see it, Mother
Superior? Tis a perfect
solution to the problem at
hand!

SISTER HONORE (O.C.)
'N' bringin' a thousand more
troubles to the table with it.

*The elderly nun struggles to get to her feet from where she has
been kneeling in prayer. Fiona offers assistance.*

FIONA
But y' said so yourself a
journey alone was too
dangerous.

SISTER HONORE
Aye.

FIONA
'N' with Daphne along to pass the time.

SISTER HONORE
I'd sooner see y' go alone.

FIONA
But she's nowhere to go.

SISTER HONORE
She has family. She can go to them.

FIONA
'N' back to the ruckus that
made her leave?

SISTER HONORE
Ruckus it is?  Another one o' those
tavern words she's been teachin'?

*Sister Honore starts toward the door, an insistent Fiona in her*
*wake.*

FIONA
She's not from a tavern, Mother
Superior.  She comes from a good
home.

SISTER HONORE
Then she should go back to it.

FIONA
But what if her destiny be
somewhere else?  Sure as y'd
want her to find it then 'n' be
gloriously happy?

SISTER HONORE
Tis the Lord's choice, Sister
Fiona.  Not ours.

*On impulse, Fiona grabs up a Bible left in the pew.*

FIONA
(thrusts it out)
Then ask Him to choose!

*The older woman looks puzzled.*

FIONA (CONT'D)
If a page were to fall open 'n'
your finger to fall on the
words of the Lord with your
eyes closed, wouldn't it be like
Himself sayin' so that then
we'd know what to do?

SISTER HONORE
'N' if it be His choice by this
way o' yours that y' not set
foot in Virginia for all your
livin' days...?

*Fiona swallows hard, unsure if she wants to go through with this.*

SISTER HONORE (CONT'D)
Well?

*Fiona takes a deep breath, splays the book open, and looks her straight in the eye. Sister Honore is surprised the young woman is going through with it but nonetheless closes her eyes, raises her index finger and brings it down on the middle of the page. She opens them to see what it says at the same moment an anxious Fiona is swiveling the book to see it, too. They look up at each other at the same time. Fiona offers a meek smile.*

EXT. THISTLEBURN ABBEY - MORNING

*Fiona and Daphne emerge from the abbey, the latter dressed in stylish traveling clothes and carrying a cape and a carpetbag. Fiona, in her habit, travels much lighter. The other SISTERS OF THISTLE whom we have not seen previously pour out the door in excitement to wave their good-byes. They range in age from 40-70, skinny ones, plump ones, tall ones, homely ones. Daphne strides to the waiting carriage. Fiona, however, is searching among the well-wishers. At last she sees*

*Sister Honore appear in the doorway with Sister Bridget behind her. She sets down her tiny bag and runs to give the Mother Superior a hug.*

FIONA
I'll be back before y' know it!

SISTER HONORE
See that y' do, lass.

*Though scowling, there is nevertheless a tear in the older woman's eyes.*

DAPHNE (O.C.)
Fiona!

FIONA
(softly)
Goodbye.

*She runs to join Fiona in the carriage. Once inside, she pokes her head out and vigorously waves to all of them again as the carriage starts to move.*

SISTER BRIDGET
(to Sister Honore)
Will she be comin' back, do y' think?

SISTER HONORE
(sadly)
They never do, Sister Bridget.
They never do.


INT. CARRIAGE - MOMENTS LATER

*POV of Fiona hanging her head out the window and watching the nuns all make their way back inside the abbey.*

*She pulls her head back inside and sees that a nonplussed
Daphne is reading a book.*

FIONA
Y' think they'll be all right?

DAPHNE
(not looking up)
Hmmm?

*Fiona gently pulls the book down.*

FIONA
The sisters?  They seemed sad
to see us go, didn't y' think?

DAPHNE
I'm sure they'll do
swimmingly.

*She starts to resume her reading.*

FIONA
I noticed y' didn't look back.

DAPHNE
What?

FIONA
As we were leavin' 'em just
now?  Y' didn't look back.

*Daphne drops the book down and looks her in the eye.*

DAPHNE
Perhaps it's because I was too
busy looking forward.
(beat)
As should you.

*As she goes back to her book, a puzzled Fiona settles back in her seat, unsure of what to make of this. She looks out the window at the passing Scottish landscape, then looks back at her traveling companion. She takes a deep sigh and crosses herself for good measure.*

*SFX: Daphne cheerfully sings A BIRD IN A GILDED CAGE.*

INT. SHIP (STEERAGE CLASS) - NIGHT

*With a PIANO PLAYER accompanying her, Daphne is entertaining the predominantly male contingent of STEERAGE CLASS PASSENGERS. They are all drinking, laughing and enjoying themselves...until a few of them happen to glance toward the door. They start to nudge one another. As the din dies down, even the pianist notices the change in tone; he, too, turns to see Fiona standing in the doorway. A few of the men cross themselves. Daphne finally notices the new arrival herself...and is not pleased by the interruption.*

FIONA
We've still a long journey for
ourselves, Daphne. Y'd best
be comin' to bed.

*A few of the men snicker at this, fueling Daphne's annoyance as she flounces off of her makeshift stage to follow the young nun.*

*SFX: Door slam*

INT. FIONA AND DAPHNE'S CABIN - MOMENTS LATER

*Once inside their cabin, Daphne proceeds to vent as she undresses and lets down her hair. Fiona, in contrast, matter of factly turns down the blanket in her tiny bunk and prepares to call it a day.*

DAPHNE
How *dare* you embarrass me like that?!

FIONA
Sure as you were doin' a fine
enough job of it yourself.

DAPHNE
I was having fun! Or is that a
bloody word you don't even
know?!

FIONA
Tis a promise I made to the Mother
Superior to keep y' from harm,
Daphne, not give y' a day pass to go
consortin' with the devil!

DAPHNE
I was *consorting* with fellow
*passengers.*

FIONA
That you were 'n' *then* some. It
isn't like I don't have eyes...

DAPHNE
You don't *own* me, Fiona
McKay!

FIONA
I never said I did.

DAPHNE
And I don't *owe* you a bloody *thing*!

FIONA
Aye...

DAPHNE
Not a single bloody farthing!

FIONA
I'd not be takin' it e'en if you <u>did</u>...

DAPHNE
Well, I don't and so there! In fact,
once we reach America, you'll
probably never see me again.

FIONA
If it be the Lord's plan for us
to be partin' company--

DAPHNE
Who *cares* about the Lord's
plan?! I'm talking about *mine*!

FIONA
Tis one 'n' the same, Daphne.
Y' just not be knowin' it yet...

*CU: Full moon*

FIONA (O.C.)
Tis a strange thing, the ways in
which y' work. 'N' I myself
not beginnin' to understand a
single word of it...


EXT. SHIP'S DECK - LATER

*Fiona is standing at the railing and looking at the stars with earnest.*

FIONA
But if y' be listenin', Lord, I
ask that y' look after the
wayward. 'N' if it not be too
much trouble, a sign perhaps
that I be doin' the right
thing...?

DAPHNE (O.C.)
What are you doing?

FIONA
(startled to have been
overheard)
Just sayin' a prayer or two.

*Daphne, wearing a cloak, approaches her.*

DAPHNE
A prayer for whom?

FIONA
For all what's be needin' it.
Nothin' more.

DAPHNE
I woke up and saw that you
weren't there.

FIONA
(shrug)
Y' needed your sleep for the
journey. I'd not be wakin' y'
with the sound o' my own
ramblin' thoughts.

*Daphne closes her hand over Fiona's in unspoken apology.*

DAPHNE
What I *need*, Fiona, is your
friendship. I can't have you
cross with me.

FIONA
'N' why would that e'er be so,
Daphne? The Lord brought y'
to us for a reason.

DAPHNE
He brought me to you because
my father is an insufferable,
controlling sonova--
(beat)
You shouldn't be out on a
night this cold.

*She removes her cloak and places it around Fiona's shoulders.*

DAPHNE (CONT'D)
Do you want me to stay with
you?

FIONA
Y' always are, lass.
(touches her chest)
Right where it counts the
most.


EXT. AMERICAN HARBOR - DAY

*Michael and Ian are eagerly awaiting Fiona's appearance on
the gangplank.*

IAN
Will y ' know her, do y' think?

MICHAEL
Sure as the day she was born,
she was the spittin' image o'
Mum.

IAN
(dumbstruck)
Holy Mother of God...

*Michael follows Ian's gaze to Daphne, now exiting the ship, the
center of male adoration. She is breathtakingly golden.
Michael takes off his cap and thwacks Ian on the shoulder.*

MICHAEL
Are y' daft, man!  Y' barely just
planted your seed in
Catherine's belly 'n' already y'
be lookin' at other women?!

IAN
I was lookin' for *you*!

MICHAEL
'N' what would myself want
with a glossy lass as that?

IAN
Sure as y' built yourself a
grand house!  What better to
be fillin' it up with the laughter
of a fine wife and a brood o'
bairn?!

MICHAEL
All in time, Ian.  All in good
time.

*Nevertheless, he hasn't taken his eyes off of Daphne.*

FIONA
(shouting)
Michael!

*Ian notices her vigorous waving before Michael does.*

IAN
(astonished)
Holy Mother of God.

*He nudges Michael and points.*

IAN (CONT'D)
You didna tell me your sister
was a sister.

MICHAEL
(with a casual shrug)
Only a little 'n' not very long.

IAN
Do y' be meanin' to change it
then?

MICHAEL
Tis America, Ian. Y' can forget
whoever y' were before 'n' start
anew.

*Fiona spots her brother and runs toward him. He swings her
in his arms in joy.*

FIONA
(laughing)
Sure as you're an even better
looker than I remember!

IAN
'N' what about myself?

*Fiona hugs him as well.*

FIONA
As if I could e'er forget!
(looks around)
Did y' bring your bride
Michael wrote of?

IAN
You'll be meeting Cate at
supper.

MICHAEL
She's a good woman.

IAN
'N' a fine cook.

MICHAEL
(smacks Ian's stomach)
As if y' couldn't tell!

FIONA
Tis your happiness that shows
the most, Ian. 'N' for that, I'm
happy for y' both.

IAN
(grins)
I got myself an angel to be
sure.

MICHAEL
(laughs)
She'd <u>have</u> to be to be puttin'
up with *this* one!  Shall we go?

*Fiona hesitates.*

FIONA
There's somethin' y' need to
know first.

MICHAEL
All I know is you're here safe
where y' *should* be.

FIONA
The passage y' sent me for a
fine cabin--

MICHAEL
Nothin' but the best, just as I
promised.

FIONA
(awkwardly)
I traded it for somethin' a little
less grand.

MICHAEL
(anxious)
Was it money y' needed then?
'Cause if it were--

FIONA
I brought a friend.
(looks to Ian, then
back to Michael)
There wasn't time to write.

MICHAEL
(laughs in relief)
'N' did y' think I'd be angry for
it?

31

FIONA
She'll be stayin' with us...just til
she finds her way.

IAN
Sure as he's plenty o' room for
a hundred!

FIONA
Y' don't mind then?

MICHAEL
(to Ian)
One o' the good sisters, no
doubt.

IAN
(looks around)
So where is she?

*Fiona turns and spies Daphne saying goodbyes to her besotted
shipmates.*

FIONA
(cups her hands to
yell)
Daphne!

*Daphne looks up, reluctantly parts from her current company
and starts walking toward them.*

IAN
Holy Mother of God...

*Michael is transfixed by her beauty. She, too, has noticed him
and offers a coy smile as she draws closer through the crowd.*

*Fiona looks at her brother, looks at the approaching Daphne, then back at Michael. She glances heavenward a moment...and smiles.*

EXT. CARRIAGE - JUST BEFORE DUSK

*Pastoral countryside outside of Alexandria, Virginia.*

DAPHNE (V.O.)
Fiona tells me that you're a
farmer, Mr. McKay.

MICHAEL (V.O.)
She should also tell y' to be
callin' me Michael. If y' like,
that is.

DAPHNE (V.O.)
So what kind of beasties do
you and Mr. Sutherland raise?

INT. CARRIAGE - CONTINUOUS

*Fiona and Daphne sit opposite Ian and Michael.*

IAN
(laughs)
Beasties, she says!

DAPHNE
Am I missing a point of
amusement?

MICHAEL
Tis tobacco we grow 'n' plenty of
it.

DAPHNE
(a raised brow)
Tobacco?

IAN
On the finest land in all o'
Virgina!

*Fiona tries unsuccessfully to stifle a yawn.*

MICHAEL
Are we keepin' y' awake, lass?

DAPHNE
(in her friend's
defense)
She's barely slept ever since
your letter arrived.

FIONA
(to Michael)
Will we be reachin' your land
soon, do y' think?

(Ian laughs.)

MICHAEL
Sure as we've been <u>on</u> it since
the last crossin'.

*Fiona sits up to look out the window.*

*Michael raps on the partition above and behind his head to signal the driver to stop.*

EXT. CARRIAGE ATOP A SLOPE

*Michael steps out first and extends his hand. Fiona tentatively sticks her head out...and is amazed. Laying before her are rows and rows of tobacco crops. And there, in the center of it, is a grand Victorian mansion. As she reaches for Michael's hand and steps out, he clearly enjoys her reaction.*

MICHAEL
Welcome home, Fiona.

*She takes a few steps forward on her own to marvel at what she is seeing. Ian hops out of the carriage next to gallantly offer his hand to Daphne. She, too, is favorably impressed by the view. She places one hand in Ian's...and offers the other to Michael as she alights.*

INT. DINING ROOM - EVENING

*Two SERVANTS discreetly remove dinner plates and refill Ian, Michael and Daphne's wine glasses. The latter's partaking of spirits is disturbing to Fiona, who sips tea, but says nothing contradictory. The fifth member of the dinner party is Ian's wife, CATHERINE, a dark-haired American (late 20's) who looks like the quintessential Gibson girl but has a sharp head for business.*

CATHERINE
So is your family still in
England, Daphne?

DAPHNE
(gayly sips her wine)
It seemed as good a place as
any to leave them.

CATHERINE
But certainly you miss them?

35

DAPHNE
(a sly grin)
As often as possible.

*Though puzzled by her remark, Catherine doesn't pursue it.*

IAN
(to Fiona)
Did I tell y' Cate here does the
books?

FIONA
Books as in writin'?

MICHAEL
Books as in numbers.
(toasts Catherine with
his wine)
She's a good head on her for
loggin' our profits.

DAPHNE
(intrigued)
And you do this as your
employment?

IAN
(laughs)
Only for us.

MICHAEL
'N' not so's anyone would
know.

CATHERINE
(leans in to Daphne)
Apparently the world's not
ready for women to assume
'manly' responsibilities.

DAPHNE
I should think Her Majesty
Queen Victoria would be
inclined to disagree.

*The two women toast each other, Daphne with her wine and
Catherine with her teacup.*

IAN
(to Catherine)
You'll have more than enough
to assume when the first bairn
comes.

CATHERINE
First...
(kisses his cheek)
...and possibly only.

*Michael and Daphne laugh, much to Ian's embarrassment.*


INT. UPSTAIRS CORRIDOR - LATER

*Michael flings open the door of a beautifully appointed
Victorian bedroom. A cautious Fiona stands at the doorway,
surveying the canopy bed with its covers turned back, an open
armoire bursting with beautiful gowns, a dressing table replete
with combs, brushes and perfume bottles. Michael gets behind
her and gives her a gentle push into the room.*


INT. FIONA'S BEDROOM - CONTINUOUS

*She takes a few steps inside but goes no further.*

MICHAEL
If the furnishin's not be to
your likin'--

FIONA
Do y' mean for *me* to stay in
this room, Michael?

MICHAEL
(looks around)
I not be seein' anyone else
layin' claim to it.

FIONA
Do y' have somethin' a wee
bit... lesser?

MICHAEL
Lesser?

FIONA
Glory be, but y' could fit all
the Sisters o' Thistle in it 'n'
they'd not be crowdin' one
another.

MICHAEL
(takes her hand)
Y' deserve it, lass, for all the
years I made y' wait in that
place.

FIONA
That place was my home,
Michael. The only one I've
known.

MICHAEL
'N' this be your home <u>now</u>.

*Eager to please her, he goes over to sit on the side of the bed.*

MICHAEL (CONT'D)
Did y' ever see as fancy a bed?

*Fiona shakes her head.*

MICHAEL (CONT'D)
(mischievously)
Watch this.

*He proceeds to bounce up and down. She laughs at the sight.*
*He stops bouncing and pats the place next to him.*

MICHAEL (CONT'D)
Come try it.

*Unsure as to whether she should, she nonetheless crosses to the*
*bed and sits down. He bounces. She bounces. He bounces*
*again. Pretty soon, they're both bouncing and laughing. She*
*finally falls back and gazes up at the canopy.*

FIONA
Oh, Michael. What have y'
come to?

MICHAEL
What I've come to is what
America's all about.

*He gets up and proceeds to wander the room as he talks,*
*admiring the dresses in the armoire and the display of crystal*
*bottles on the dressing table.*

MICHAEL
Tis a place where a man can
be what he wants, sure as he's
willin' to pay for it in a good
sweat 'n' a lot o' dreams. Y'
not be findin' that kind o'
fortune where we come from,

Fiona. Not when y' be doin'
the same thing from cradle to
grave 'n' ne'er seein' past your
next debt 'n' your next empty
plate. Y'd be too young too
remember the bad times,
Fiona, but I saw what the lack
o' hope did to Mum and Da 'n'
I swore I'd be doin' better by
'em, not just for me, y' know,
but for the both of us. "Look
after Fiona," they said, 'n' that
I've done by keepin' the
promise I made when Ian 'n'
myself took leave o' the sod to
come here. 'N all that I ask--

*He turns to see that Fiona has fallen fast asleep while he was
talking. He gently repositions her so that her head is on the
pillow and pulls a blanket over her. He kisses her forehead
and smiles fondly.*

MICHAEL
(softly)
All that I ask is that y' just be
givin' it a chance.


INT. FOYER - MOMENTS LATER

*Ian and Catherine are leaving for the evening. As Ian gets
their cloaks, Catherine takes Daphne aside.*

CATHERINE
It's written on his face, plain as
day.

DAPHNE
(laughs)
And what would I be wanting
with a farmer?

CATHERINE
A *successful* farmer, Daphne.
Not to mention a man who's
spent far too much time by
himself. You could do a lot
worse.

DAPHNE
Perhaps I already have...

*Michael has just come down the stairs and noticed their
impending departure.*

MICHAEL
Y' not be leaving already?

IAN
Catie's a wee bit tired.

CATHERINE
Oh, go on with you!  I wasn't
the one falling asleep in the
gooseberry pie...

IAN
Sure as y' be mistakin' me for
Fiona.

DAPHNE
(to Michael)
Is she all right?

MICHAEL
Aye but she's as hearty a stock
as the McKay's come by.
She'll be herself again by the
morn.

*Catherine moves in to give Daphne a hug goodbye.*

CATHERINE
I hope that you'll be staying
long enough for us to become
good friends.

DAPHNE
It was already assured within
the first five minutes.

*Daphne extends her hand to Ian.*

DAPHNE (CONT'D)
You've a very fine wife, Mr.
Sutherland.

IAN
Aye, that she be, Miss Hedges.

*Daphne turns to Michael and smiles.*

DAPHNE
Mr. McKay.

*He nods awkwardly and watches her glide past them and up the stairs.*

CATHERINE
Hmmm...

IAN
Hmmm?

MICHAEL
'N' what are the two o' you
hummin' about?

*Ian looks to Catherine who simply smiles.*

IAN
Y' could do a lot worse, y'
know.

MICHAEL
(wistfully)
Aye.

*SFX: Rooster crowing*


EXT. TOBACCO PLANTATION - EARLY
MORNING

*WORKERS are already tending to the crops.*


INT. DAPHNE'S BEDROOM

*Daphne POV as she looks through her bedroom window at the workers.*

DAPHNE
Oh, Mr. McKay. Why the bloody hell
did your farm have to go and be
tobacco?


INT. DINING ROOM - MOMENTS LATER

*CU of a property map, the sides of which are held down with cups of coffee.*

IAN (O.C.)
Why are y' gettin' your
knickers in a knot for 20
parcels? We'd hardly miss it,
I'm tellin' y'.

MICHAEL (O.C.)
Have y' learned nothin' since
we came here, Ian? They're
leeches sure as the day is long!
Give 'em an inch 'n' they'll
take a mile o' good land.

*Ian and Michael have taken a break from breakfast to study
their maps.*

IAN
Aye but only if the land knows
how to <u>yield</u>. Y' said yourself-
-

MICHAEL
What I said myself is we let
'em sit 'n' wait.

IAN
'N' what if they lose interest?

MICHAEL
(laughs)
In a soil that ripe o' profit?
They'd be cuttin' their nose to
spite their butt-ugly faces!

*Ian goes to pick up his coffee, causing the map to immediately
roll up on itself. As he and Michael go to straighten it, Fiona-
-still wearing her nun's habit--appears in the doorway. She
politely coughs so as not to startle them.*

44

IAN
Mornin', Fiona.

*Michael looks her up and down in amusement.*

MICHAEL
Just look at y' now, lass. 'N'
still wearing last night's
clothes.

*She looks down a moment at her habit.*

MICHAEL (CONT'D)
Not to worry.  We'll not be
lettin' your meal get cold while
y' run up 'n' freshen for the
day.

FIONA
Aye but I already did.

MICHAEL
(puzzled)
But your--uh--
(off habit)
--thing y' be wearin'--

FIONA
Tis what I *always* wear,
Michael.  Y' didn't know that?

MICHAEL
Aye but that was *then*, Fiona.
This is *now*.

FIONA
Aye. 'N' this is who I *am*.
Forever.

*Michael looks to Ian for support. Ian, however, merely shrugs.*


EXT. PLANTATION - LATER

*Michael and Ian are, respectively, giving Daphne and Fiona a
tour of the land. The pairs are far apart enough so as not to
hear each other's conversations.*

MICHAEL
(to Daphne)
So y' know my sister well,
would y' say?

DAPHNE
As well as the next, I suppose.

MICHAEL
So when she says 'forever'...?

DAPHNE
Yes?

MICHAEL
Would y' have any idea what
she means exactly?

DAPHNE
(shrug)
The rest of her life?

                                        CUT TO:


IAN
So this friend o' yours?

FIONA
Daphne?

IAN
Was she plannin' to take the
veil same as yourself?

FIONA
(laughs)
Sure as y' be makin' a joke,
Ian.

IAN
Y' said she was sharin' the
abbey roof when first y' met.

FIONA
Much to the discomfort o' the
Mother Superior.

IAN
'N' how was that?

FIONA
She's a free spirit, our Daphne.
'N' not one to be bowin' to
common convention.

IAN
But her heart, y' think, would
it be free to love?

FIONA
(knowingly)
Only if the right man made a
move in the proper time.


INT. COURTYARD - LATER

*Ian and Michael watch Fiona and Daphne happily strolling
the grounds. Ian is lighting a pipe.*

MICHAEL
So?

IAN
So y'd best be makin' your
move 'n' good haste to it.

MICHAEL
Hmmm...

IAN
'N' what of Fiona?

MICHAEL
(shakes his head)
It'd seem the Lord moved
first.

HIS PUFF OF PIPE SMOKE DISSOLVES
TO:

INT. BOARD ROOM - DAY

*CU of smoke emanating from the pipe of CORNELIUS PIERPONT (60's), a tobacco executive in Alexandria.*

*Piermont and a board room full of straight-laced and stuffy BUSINESSMEN, including HARRY GRIGGS and LIONEL BLOUNT (both in their 40's), are discussing recent attempts to acquire a particular plantation. The majority of them are smoking.*

PIERPONT
They're amateurs, gentlemen.
They don't know how to play
the game.

BUSINESSMAN 1
Then why are they winning?

*This elicits a few chuckles around the room.*

PIERPONT
They're not winning by any
stroke of the imagination.
We're simply waiting them
out.

BLOUNT
We've been waiting them out
for 3 years.

BUSINESSMAN 2
And without result.

PIERPONT
Achilles, gentlemen. It's all a
matter of Achilles.

GRIGGS
Which one is Achilles? A new
partner?

PIERPONT
Your lack of classical
education betrays you, Griggs.

*More snickers around the room.*

PIERPONT (CONT'D)
For the rest of you who may
be similarly unenlightened,
Achilles was a Greek whose
mother held him by the heel
and dipped him into the
waters of immortality.

BLOUNT
What's that to do with forcing
the Scots to sell?

PIERPONT
Every man has a weakness. A
point of vulnerability that will
compel him to yield. Even
our esteemed chairman--and
this is strictly confidential
among us--has been known to
demonstrate an occasional
lapse of judgment insofar as
circumstances of--shall we say-
-personal challenge?

BLOUNT
What's your point, Pierpont?

GRIGGS
Blount is right. What does any
of this have to do with
acquisition?

*As Pierpont replies, the camera pulls out, through the window,
down the side of the building, and down to King Street.*

PIERPONT (O.S.)
Simply stated, gentlemen, we
must find out what would
wound our thick-headed Scots
the most...and strike when the
opportunity best presents
itself.


EXT. KING STREET - CONTINUOUS

*Catherine and Daphne are leisurely strolling and shopping.
Like a veritable Red Sea parting, every male on the sidewalk
gallantly steps aside with a tip of the hat to allow them to pass.*

DAPHNE
There's certainly no shortage
of friendliness, is there?

CATHERINE
That surprises you?

DAPHNE
Quite frankly, I didn't know
<u>what</u> to expect.

CATHERINE
And yet you came anyway?

DAPHNE
Fiona can be very persuasive.

CATHERINE
Really?

DAPHNE
That and Sister Bridget wanted
to throw me out on my tush if
I didn't go back to my family.

CATHERINE
(awkwardly)
The other night--if I was
forward at all in--

DAPHNE
--asking about them?  Not in
the slightest.

51

CATHERINE
No?

DAPHNE
My father promised me to a
man who was twice my age
and who looked like a hippo in
a waistcoat.

CATHERINE
I take it you had no affection
for him?

DAPHNE
We'd only met twice and both
times I found him to be
completely tedious.

CATHERINE
And so you ran away?

DAPHNE
Given my circumstances, it
seemed like a reasonable
progression. After all, isn't
America the land of the free?

CATHERINE
And you don't worry they'll
find you and take you back?

DAPHNE
Not if they haven't the
foggiest where to even <u>look</u>.

*Laughing, the two of them enter a millinery.*


EXT. VERANDA - AFTERNOON

*Fiona is gazing out on the plantation. Michael is settled, hip-shot on the railing.*

MICHAEL
It was kind o' y' to be givin'
the gowns to Daphne.

FIONA
Sure as they suit her well.

MICHAEL
Would y' like me to call 'round
the dress mistress to sew y' up
some more?

FIONA
Seems as if America made y'
frivolous, Michael.

MICHAEL
Not when it comes to what y'
want, lass.

FIONA
What I want or what y' want
for yourself? I was content
long before y' sent for me.

MICHAEL
'N' now y' can be even <u>more</u>
content.

FIONA
How so?

MICHAEL
Name what y' want and it's
yours.

FIONA
What I *want* is for y' to stop
tellin' me what I want.

MICHAEL
Done.

FIONA
Good.

MICHAEL
So what does Daphne want,
do y' think?

FIONA
That's for yourself to find out.

INT. KITCHEN - LATER

*CU of the fixings of a fabulous meal being prepped by
Michael's gregarious African American cook, DELIAH
(40's)*

*Fiona sits on a stool, fascinated by this entire process. In a
style worthy of a Beni-Hana chef, Deliah expertly chops a
carrot and flips a piece to Fiona, who excitedly catches it and
pops it into her mouth.*

DELIAH
(amused)
That gonna keep you til
supper, hon?

FIONA
(admiring the
impending feast)
Sure as it's some kind o' magic
y' do, Deliah!

DELIAH
Ain't no magic but keepin'
them that's hungry from belly-
achin' I ain't put out 'nuff
food.

FIONA
(marveling)
Tis more than could feed an
army o' Scots against
Longshanks.

DELIAH
Shanks who?

FIONA
It's a long story.
(off food)
Do y' really mean for us to eat
all o' this?

DELIAH
Lawdy you ain't seen nothin'!
This just a <u>regular</u> meal.
Come Christmas, Mister
McKay, he done spread it on
thick 'n' fine like one o' them
fancy-pants royals.

FIONA
Does he now?

DELIAH
And the lights? Mmm, mmm,
mmm. I says to him, "Mister
McKay," I says, "you done
gone 'n' put up so many
'round the house, they gonna
see it clear from the moon!"

FIONA
Tis a shame I'll be missin' it.

DELIAH
(with a scowl)
What you say?

CUT TO:

INT. MICHAEL'S STUDY - LATER

*Michael is pacing the room, flustered by the news he's heard.*

MICHAEL
Scotland?!

FIONA
Tis the only home I know.

MICHAEL
Til *now*!

FIONA
'N' why should 'now' make a
bit o' difference?

MICHAEL
I brought y' here--

FIONA
Y' brought me here to show--
(corrects herself)
--to *boast* how well you've
done for yourself.

MICHAEL
'N' to *share* it!

FIONA
Sure as you've got a good
heart, Michael. Y' always
have. But I'd not be makin' y'
part with somethin' I never
asked for.

MICHAEL
(folds his arms)
I'll not be payin' for your
passage back.

FIONA
(folds her arms)
Then I'd best be learnin' to
swim.

*SFX: Knock on open door.*

*Both look up to see Daphne standing there.*

DAPHNE
Do you suppose the two of
you could postpone your
quarrel until after we've dined?

MICHAEL
(spontaneously)
Settle somethin' for us,
Daphne.

DAPHNE
Settle what?

MICHAEL
Outa the blue, Fiona here
plans to be takin' leave of us.

DAPHNE
(puzzled)
We've only just arrived.

FIONA
Aye, but--

MICHAEL
But nothin'!  After all the
trouble--

DAPHNE
You could at least show the
courtesy to let her finish.

*Grudgingly, Michael allows Fiona to have the floor.*

FIONA
Y' don't understand.  I need to
go where I'm needed.

MICHAEL
(insistent)
I need y' *here*.

FIONA
Not as much as the *sisters* need
be *there*.

*Michael turns to Daphne for resolution.*

MICHAEL
Well?

DAPHNE
You're a grown up woman,
Fiona.  You should go
wherever it is that makes you

happiest...and not let anyone
tell you differently.

*Fiona grins.*

MICHAEL
(exasperated)
Do y' call that tryin' to help?

DAPHNE
I call it being honest.

MICHAEL
(smugly)
Then try *this* 'honest' on for
size. How's she supposed to
pay passage if I don't give her
the money?

*Daphne purposefully strolls up to him. She snaps off one
garnet earring and then the other and holds them face-up in the
palm of her hand.*

DAPHNE
By selling these.

*Intrigued to examine their value, he reaches for one. She
quickly snaps her hand shut and gives them to Fiona. She
then smiles, flips her hair and flounces out of the room.*

*Fiona, impressed with such display, smiles at her brother, flips
her veil, and imitates Daphne's flouncing exit. Which, of
course, on a nun looks rather silly.*


EXT. TOBACCO PLANTATION - EVENING

*A starry sky, tall trees, a perfect night.*

FIONA (O.C.)
I don't mean to be soundin'
harsh or ungrateful, y' know.
As scared as I was to be
comin' so far from home, y'
got me here safe 'n' without
incident 'n' for that I give
thanks. But sure as y' can see
the hardship I left behind 'n'
why it wouldn't be right to
break my promise. If y' really
mean for me to *stay* here,
though, then I ask y' to give
me a sign 'n' show me the way
a little clearer.

MICHAEL (O.C.)
What are you doin'?

FIONA
(startled to have been
overheard)
Just sayin' a prayer or two.

*Michael approaches her.*

MICHAEL
A prayer for whom?

FIONA
For all what's be needin' it.
Nothin' more.

MICHAEL
About the things I said--

FIONA
Y' spoke your heart, Michael.
I'd not be faultin' y' for it. Just

as I'd not be wantin' yourself
to be mad at me for the same.

MICHAEL
If y' could just give it a bit
more time...?

FIONA
Time is somethin' they're
runnin' out of, I'm afraid.

MICHAEL
Who?

FIONA
The good sisters y' left me
with. They're not young
women anymore. How do y'
expect 'em to get by if I don't
go back?

MICHAEL
Y' can't do it all, Fiona. Why
can't y' see that?

FIONA
(shakes her head)
Y' may as well be talkin' to the
wind. My mind is made
up...with or without your
blessin', much as I'd like to
have it.

*She sadly turns away from him.*

MICHAEL
If it's money y'd be havin' me
send them...?

FIONA
It isn't money they be needin',
not when they've been
through so much without it.

MICHAEL
Are y' <u>sure</u> that goin' back is
the only solution?

*Fiona heaves a heavy sigh and, as she does so, she happens to look up at the house. With lights warmly burning in every window, it suddenly seems much larger to her than it was before.*

MICHAEL (CONT'D)
Fiona?

*She turns to him, tilts her head, and smiles.*

EXT. THISTLEBURN ABBEY - MORNING

*CU of male hand knocking on the door of the abbey. It is opened by Sister Bridget. A breathless Seamus eagerly thrusts a letter into her hands.*

SEAMUS
A letter from America, Sister
Bridget. Do y' think it's from
Sister Fiona?

SISTER BRIDGET
Hmmm...

*She contemplates it a moment before turning and closing the door, much to Seamus' disappointment.*

*CU of elderly hands slowly unfolding the letter.*

INT. THISTLEBURN ABBEY - LATER

*The hands are those of the Mother Superior. As she reads the contents, an anxious Sister Bridget stands on the other side of the desk awaiting her reaction. Sister Honore finishes, sets the pages down, and removes her spectacles, still not saying a word. Unable to contain herself any longer, Sister Bridget blurts out a prompt.*

SISTER BRIDGET
Well?

SISTER HONORE
Well what?

SISTER BRIDGET
(off letter)
Quite a surprise, don't y'
think?

SISTER HONORE
Aye, Sister Bridget. That it
was.

SISTER BRIDGET
Sincere as well. She'd not be
askin' if she didn't mean it.

SISTER HONORE
Aye. It's not her way.

*Sister Bridget shifts from one foot to the next, impatient for the Mother Superior to say more. With glacial slowness, Sister Honore puts her glasses back on to read the letter a second time.*

SISTER BRIDGET
Well?

*Sister Honore looks at her over the rim of her glasses.*

SISTER HONORE
Have y' shared this yet with
any o' the others?

SISTER BRIDGET
(awkwardly)
Only one or two.

*Sister Honore looks past her to the doorway. Unbeknownst to
Sister Bridget, a quorum of nuns are all eagerly hovering to see
what the response to the letter will be. Sister Bridget follows the
Mother Superior's gaze. Embarrassed, she turns back to her
and leans in confidentially.*

SISTER BRIDGET
Y' know how they can't keep a
secret...

SISTER HONORE
Aye.

*There is a long, uncomfortable silence.*

SISTER BRIDGET
What will y' be writin' back to her?

SISTER HONORE
(solemnly)
Y' can't just up 'n' leave a place
that's always been home.
(to the rest)
Y' should know that by now.

*The other nuns hang their heads in embarrassment for daring to
think outside the box.*

SISTER HONORE (CONT'D)
What would be happenin', do
y' think, if every shepherd up

'n' decided to abandon his
flock just to be movin' on to
somewhere else?

*No one knows how to answer this. Except Sister Bridget.*

SISTER BRIDGET
(tentatively)
He could be tendin' to a <u>new</u>
flock in the somewhere else...

*The doorway nuns brighten somewhat at this and look earnestly
to their leader. Sister Honore reluctantly realizes she is
outnumbered.*

SISTER HONORE
Tisn't a level o' question for
ourselves to be decidin'.
(beat)
I'll put the matter to Father
Patrick 'n' see what <u>he</u> says.

*Renewed with hope, the nuns grin and enthusiastically cross
themselves.*

*SFX: Church bells*


INT. THISTLEBURN PARISH - EVENING

*CU of a saucer of milk being transported by a pair of elderly
male hands.*

*CU of feet in worn shoes poking out beneath a wool robe as
their owner ploddingly shuffles across the floor to the front door.*


I/E. THISTLEBURN PARISH - CONTINUOUS

*The door opens to reveal FATHER PATRICK (70's), the parish priest of this community. Although the years have slowed him down, he's jovial, kind-hearted, and really believes that his cats understand everything he says. As he bends down to put the saucer of milk on the step, his feline pets come from all directions.*

FATHER PATRICK
There y' go, kitties.  Drink
hearty.

*As he proceeds to fondly stroke the new arrivals, his glance falls on an envelope that has been propped up for him to see.*

FATHER PATRICK (CONT'D)
'N' what have we here?

*The cats meow in response.*

FATHER PATRICK (CONT'D)
A letter, is it, y' say?
(peers closely)
'N' from the Mother Superior
it seems.
(queries cats)
Now what do y' suppose she's
writin' us for, hmm?

*The cats meow.*

FATHER PATRICK (CONT'D)
Aye.  Let's open it 'n' see.

*He turns to take the letter inside.  A few of the cats follow him in.  As he takes it to his desk and sits down to open it, they proceed to leap up on the surface, roll around on his papers and just generally act as if they own the place.  He shakes his head in dismay upon finishing it.*

FATHER PATRICK (CONT'D)
(clucks his tongue as
he strokes the nearest
cat)
Tch, tch, tch. We've got
ourselves a pickle, Mrs.
Whiskers.

*She meows.*

FATHER PATRICK (CONT'D)
Y' can say that again. The
trouble is what do y' think I
should do?

*She meows again.*

FATHER PATRICK (CONT'D)
(with a smile)
Aye. The Bishop Campbell would
know.

*He reaches for a quill.*

FATHER PATRICK (CONT'D)
I'll write to him straightaway.


EXT. PRINCES STREET, EDINBURGH - DAY

TITLE CARD: EDINBURGH


INT. BISHOP CAMPBELL'S OFFICE -
CONTINUOUS

*CU of a male hand (STEVEN, a clerk) holding out a letter.*

STEVEN (O.C.)
An urgent letter from the
parish priest at Thistleburn,
Your Excellency.

*BISHOP CAMPBELL (50's) looks up from his reading.*

BISHOP CAMPBELL
(reaches for it in
concern)
Father Patrick?

STEVEN
It'd seem he's had an odd
request 'n' seeks your advice.

*Steven patiently waits as the Bishop reads the contents.*

BISHOP CAMPBELL
Hmm...

*He sets the letter down a moment.*

STEVEN
Do y' need me to be takin' a
letter?

BISHOP CAMPBELL
Aye.

*Steven efficiently opens an ornate wooden box on the Bishop's
desk and withdraws a sheet of paper, an inkwell, and a quill.*

BISHOP CAMPBELL (CONT'D)
It'll be to His Grace in
London.

STEVEN
(puzzled)
The Archbishop Greenleaf?

BISHOP CAMPBELL
(wisely)
*He'll* know what to do.

SFX: Big Ben chiming the start of the evening hour.


EXT. LONDON - DUSK

TITLE CARD: LONDON


INT. CATHEDRAL - CONTINUOUS

*The English ARCHBISHOP GREENLEAF (60's) is*
*conferring with TWO CLERICS when his clerk,*
*ANDREW, breathlessly rushes up, carrying a letter.*

ANDREW
A thousand pardons, Your
Grace, but this just came for
you from His Excellency
Bishop Campbell in
Edinburgh.

*As he takes the letter from Andrew and looks to the two men,*
*they bow their heads in understanding the meeting has come to a*
*close and discreetly withdraw. The Archbishop opens the letter*
*as Andrew hovers, awaiting further instruction.*

ARCHBISHOP GREENLEAF
Hmm...

ANDREW
Disturbing news from
Scotland, Your Excellency?

ARCHBISHOP GREENLEAF
I shall need to confer with a
higher authority before reply.
Fetch your writing materials,
Andrew. I must get word of
this at once to His Eminence
Cardinal LeSage.

*SFX: Morning birds*

EXT. FRENCH CATHEDRAL - MORNING

TITLE CARD: PARIS

EXT. COURTYARD BEHIND THE
CATHEDRAL - CONTINUOUS

*The French CARDINAL LESAGE (60's) is leisurely
strolling the gardens. A bevy of dutiful NUNS are traveling
in his wake. As he pauses to smell a rose, SISTER MARIE
comes up to him with a letter. The following scene is in French
with subtitles.*

SISTER MARIE
Blessings of the bountiful
morning, Your Eminence.

CARDINAL LESAGE
Blessings of the morning to
you as well, Sister Marie.

SISTER MARIE
Forgive the interruption on
your solitude.

CARDINAL LESAGE
But, of course.  What is it?

SISTER MARIE
(hands him letter)
A most urgent matter from
His Excellency Archbishop
Greenleaf in London.

*He takes the letter, opens it and scowls as he reads.*

NUNS
(in unison)
Bad news, Your Eminence?

CARDINAL LESAGE
A most peculiar matter seems
to have arisen in Scotland. It
involves an order of nuns.

NUNS
(in unison)
Nuns, Your Eminence?

CARDINAL LESAGE
It appears they wish to
abandon their current order
and re-establish themselves in
a place called Virginia.

SISTER MARIE
(seeking to enlighten
herself)
Was Virginia not named for
our Holy Savior, Your
Eminence?

CARDINAL LESAGE
Hmmm...I believe that it was.

NUNS
(in unison)
Such a dilemma!  What will
you do?

CARDINAL LESAGE
(considers this a
moment)
It is a question I am not
worthy to answer.  I shall
dispatch at once a letter to His
Holiness, the Pope.

The nuns all solemnly bow their heads and cross
themselves.

CARDINAL LESAGE (CONT'D)
He will know what to do.


EXT. THE VATICAN - DUSK

*SFX: Brisk footsteps.*


INT. THE POPE'S QUARTERS - CONTINUOUS

*A set of double doors are opened by VATICAN GUARDS. A male PRIVATE SECRETARY enters, clutching a letter.*

*POV behind a head wearing a gold and white miter. This scene is in Italian with subtitles.*

PRIVATE SECRETARY
Forgive the intrusion, Your
Holiness.

THE POPE (O.C.)
What is it that brings you in
such haste, Angelo?

PRIVATE SECRETARY
It is a letter delivered today
from His Eminence Cardinal
LeSage.

THE POPE (O.C.)
Is there trouble in France?

PRIVATE SECRETARY
No. He writes to you because
of a letter he received from
His Grace Archbishop
Greenleaf.

THE POPE (O.C.)
Is that to say, then, that there
are storms of discontent in
London?

PRIVATE SECRETARY
(shakes his head)
No, His Grace states that he
received correspondence from

His Excellency Bishop
Campbell of Edinburgh.

THE POPE (O.C.)
I am getting seriously
confused. Is there a problem
at the root of all of this?

PRIVATE SECRETARY
Nuns, Your Holiness.

THE POPE (O.C.)
Nuns?

PRIVATE SECRETARY
The Sisters of Thistle, a small
order in the Highlands of
Scotland. It seems they wish
to go to America.

THE POPE (O.C.)
Hmm.

PRIVATE SECRETARY
His Grace felt that such a
decision must be made at the
highest level.

THE POPE (O.C.)
In other words, he did not
wish to make the decision
himself?

PRIVATE SECRETARY
It would appear so, yes.

THE POPE (O.C.)
Nuns, you say?

PRIVATE SECRETARY
Yes?

THE POPE (O.C.)
How many?

PRIVATE SECRETARY
Two dozen, perhaps less.

THE POPE (O.C.)
And it is their plan to continue
the order in their adopted
land?

PRIVATE SECRETARY
Yes, Your Holiness.  That is
what has been related in the
letters that preceded this one.
(beat)
If I might speak candidly?

THE POPE (O.C.)
But of course.

PRIVATE SECRETARY
Its flock of followers has been
diminishing.  In a word, Your
Holiness, its continued
purpose is unclear to many.

THE POPE (O.C.)
Then perhaps it is time for
them to ministrate to a *new*
flock.

PRIVATE SECRETARY
Do you mean?

THE POPE (O.C.)
Yes.
(beat)
Tell them that they are free to
go.


EXT. AMERICAN HARBOR - MORNING

*Michael and Fiona are watching the passengers get off the newly arrived ship. Fiona is beside herself with excitement.*

FIONA
Sure as it's a dream come true!

MICHAEL
Or a nightmare...

FIONA
Did y' know it was the Pope
himself gave his blessin' for
them to come?

MICHAEL
Talk about havin' friends in high
places...

*Fiona looks heavenward, knowingly.*

FIONA
Aye, that they do.

*The entourage of nuns, looking not unlike an assembly of chattering, bobblehead penguins, suddenly emerge from the ship. Fiona excitedly pushes her way forward to greet them, all the while keeping an eye out for a sign of Sister Bridget and the Mother Superior. It soon becomes apparent, however, that they are not there, forcing Fiona to keep a stiff upper lip as she makes introductions to her brother.*

MICHAEL
(to Fiona)
Is that all of 'em then?

*In despair, Fiona glances back at the gangplank just in time to see Sister Bridget and a CREW MEMBER assisting the very frail Sister Honore. Fiona smiles, crosses herself and looks heavenward.*

FIONA
(quietly)
Praise be to the Lord.


INT. DINING ROOM - LATE AFTERNOON

*Ian, Daphne and Catherine (whose pregnancy is now showing) are playing poker. Ian smokes a pipe; he and Daphne are both drinking wine. Ian chuckles as he lays down his hand.*

IAN
Read 'em 'n' weep.

*He starts to reach for Daphne's stack of chips. She smacks his hand with her own fan of cards.*

DAPHNE
If there's any crying to be
done, it certainly won't be me.

*She tosses her cards on the table, displaying a better hand.*

IAN
(with an arghghgh of
annoyance)
Do y' never get tired o'
winnin'?

DAPHNE
Not really.

CATHERINE
(sweetly)
Nor your wife, Mr. Sutherland.

*Holding her cards to her chin and fluttering them like a seductive Spanish fan, she displays her hand, which beats both of theirs. She and Daphne laugh.*

IAN
I should never have taught y'
the game.

*SFX: Front door opening and commotion in the foyer.*

*The three of them exchange a look.*

CATHERINE
Back already?
(to Ian)
What time is it?

*Ian pulls out his pocketwatch.*

DAPHNE
Time really *does* fly when
you're having fun.

*Ian smirks at her.*

## INT. FOYER/CORRIDOR - CONTINUOUS

*Ian with his pipe, Daphne with her glass of wine, and Catherine fanning herself with the cards step out just as the gaggle of awestruck nuns are walking by. The latter stop to stare at this hedonistic trio, crossing themselves and smiling nervously. Fiona breaks through the group, excited to show them the rest of their new home.*

FIONA
(off the trio)
I'll be makin' introductions
later after you've rested from
your journey.

*As she moves off down the corridor, they proceed to follow her, marveling all the while at the furnishings, art, high ceilings. Ian, Daphne and Catherine watch them go, unaware that Michael and Sister Bridget, on either side of Sister Honore, have just entered.*

CATHERINE
(to Ian and Daphne)
Did you know there'd be so
many?

DAPHNE
And all under one roof.

IAN
Aye but that rips it. We've
died 'n' gone to Hell.

*Daphne happens to glance back and see her two former adversaries.*

DAPHNE
(as she taps Ian on the
arm)
Not yet but probably soon.

*Ian, Catherine and Daphne put on their best fake smiles.*

INT. UPSTAIRS CORRIDOR - MOMENTS
LATER

*Fiona grandly flings open the door to one of the bedrooms and
gently prods them to step inside and look at it.*

INT. BEDROOM - CONTINUOUS

*Like children in a candy store, they're all too dazzled to know
what to touch or look at first. Fiona stands back and enjoys
their thrill of discovery. Two of the nuns approach the bed,
touch it, sit on the edge, and are pleased by its bounceability.
Several of the others rush over to join in.*

*SISTER JOSEPHINE, a meeker member of the order, tugs
on Fiona's sleeve.*

SISTER JOSEPHINE
(in a polite whisper)
If y' mean for all of us to be sharin'
the one room, Sister Fiona, we
might be needin' a few more beds.

FIONA
(laughs)
Not to worry yourself, Sister
Josephine. There'll be two of
y' to a room 'n' plenty o' space
to go 'round.

SISTER JOSEPHINE
(astonished by this, she
remarks confidentially)
Sure as in a place like this a
body could forget about its
vows o' poverty!

INT. UPSTAIRS CORRIDOR/BEDROOM -
MOMENTS LATER

*POV Mother Superior as Fiona opens another bedroom door.*

FIONA
I remembered how partial y'
were to the mornin' sun at
Thistleburn.

*She strides across to the window and parts the draperies.*

FIONA (CONT'D)
It isn't quite the view but I
thought y'd like it all the same.

*With Sister Bridget's assistance, Sister Honore makes her way
into the room, not sure she approves of the trappings of excess.
She reaches the window and looks out on the expansive view of
the plantation. Fiona anxiously awaits the older woman's
reaction. Sister Honore finally turns and nods.*

SISTER HONORE
It'll do, Sister Fiona. It'll do
just fine.


EXT. VERANDA - EVENING

*Daphne is strolling by herself. Michael has just stepped out in
search of her. Though pleased to see her, he's suddenly self-
conscious that they are alone.*

MICHAEL
So...

DAPHNE
So?

MICHAEL
I--uh--take it a few of 'em
aren't fond o' seein' y' here?

DAPHNE
They weren't fond of seeing
me there, either.

MICHAEL
Would it be impertinent o' me
to ask why?

DAPHNE
It would. But I'll answer you
anyway.  I don't like living in a
place with so many rules.

MICHAEL
Aye, but they're not a bad
thing sometimes.  Rules, that
is.

DAPHNE
I also don't like being told
how I'm to live my life and
who I'm to marry.

MICHAEL
(confused)
Fiona said they wanted y' to
join the order.  Wouldn't your
marryin' someone be off the
plate to begin with?

*Daphne realizes she has let more information slip than she
wished.  To cover for it, she scrambles up another "in-your-face"
declaration, a move that brings her dangerously close to
Michael.*

DAPHNE
And I *also* don't like the feeling
of constantly being *watched*!

*This sudden proximity is more than he could hope for. At the
very same moment, however, they realize they are being watched.
They turn to see half a dozen nuns watching from the window.
The moment of magic is lost.*


INT. DINING ROOM - MORNING

*Michael comes into the dining room to find Fiona eating by
herself.*

MICHAEL
Late sleepers, are they?

FIONA
What?

MICHAEL
Where are your friends?

FIONA
(laugh)
Sure as y'd have to get up
earlier than this to catch 'em.

MICHAEL
Meanin' what?

FIONA
They're puttin' themselves to
good use.


*MONTAGE:*

*Some of the nuns are in the field trying to help with the tobacco crop. The existing workers are dubious of their presence.*

*A handful of nuns are in the kitchen watching Deliah. They try to offer help but she's not amenable to sharing her kitchen.*

*The rest of the nuns are walking down King Street in Alexandria. The curious PASSERS-BY give them a wide berth, unsure of what to make of them. The camera travels up the side of the building they have just passed to:*

INT. BOARD ROOM - CONTINUOUS

*Pierpont, Griggs and Blount are leaning out the window watching them go past.*

PIERPONT
Nuns?

BLOUNT
They appear to be the real
thing.

GRIGGS
Why the hell would they bring
nuns to the plantation?

PIERPONT
Isn't it obvious, gentlemen?

*Apparently not to the two of them.*

PIERPONT (CONT'D)
They intend to replace their
regular workers with cheap
labor and reduce their
operating costs.

BLOUNT AND GRIGGS
Hmm...

PIERPONT
We may have underestimated
them.


INT. DRAWING ROOM - DAY

*A very pregnant Catherine is knitting baby things as Fiona is
reading to her. Michael paces.*

MICHAEL
I don't know, Fiona.  Do y'
really think it's workin' out?

FIONA
Just as I said it would.  If it's
one thing they know how to
do, it's blend in.

*MONTAGE:*

*The plantation workers and the nuns are industriously working
side by side and having a good time of it.*

*Deliah is taking earnest instruction from the nuns who have
taken over her kitchen and are showing her how to add spices.*

*In Alexandria, the nuns are being enthusiastically greeted by
the townspeople as they go about their errands.*


INT. NEWSPAPER OFFICE - MORNING

*An EDITOR and REPORTER stand at the window as the
nuns go by.  Struck by simultaneous inspiration, they turn to
each other.*

EDITOR
Now *there's* a story you could
do!

REPORTER
Now *there's* a story I could do!


INT. DINING ROOM - MORNING

*Michael, having breakfast with Ian and Fiona, is astonished at a local newspaper item.*

MICHAEL
Who'd have thought?

FIONA
Thought what?

MICHAEL
(hands her the paper)
They seem to have made a stir.

*CU of headline: Doers of Good Deeds Call Alexandria "Home"*

FIONA
(pleased)
Aye, that they did.

*SFX: Daphne singing in the distance.*

*The three listen for a moment.  Michael leans toward Fiona.*

MICHAEL
About your friend Daphne.
There's somethin' I've been
meanin' to say--

FIONA
It's her singin', isn't it?

MICHAEL
What?

FIONA
I'll tell her to stop
straightaway.

MICHAEL
No, no, it isn't that at all.

FIONA
What then?

*He starts to open his mouth but realizes Ian hangs on every word.*

MICHAEL
(to Ian)
Haven't y' somewhere to be?

IAN
Not really.


INT. DAPHNE'S BEDROOM - LATER

*Fiona is watching Daphne at her dressing table.*

DAPHNE
Plans?

FIONA
(with difficulty)
When first y' came with me,
Daphne, I couldn't say no.

DAPHNE
As I recall, it was your idea.

FIONA
'N' a fine idea it was, too.  I'm
not sayin' it wasn't.

DAPHNE
Then what *are* you saying?

FIONA
Seein' as how a few months
have passed 'n' all--

DAPHNE
(awareness dawning)
I think I know where this is
going.

FIONA
Y' do?

DAPHNE
He wants me to leave, doesn't
he?

FIONA
Who?

DAPHNE
Your brother.

FIONA
(laughs)
Far from it, y' know.  Quite
the opposite, in fact.

DAPHNE
(intrigued)
Really?

INT. DINING ROOM - EVENING

*CU of a bountiful Thanksgiving feast*

SISTER JOSEPHINE (O.C.)
'N' for the good health 'n'
continued salvation o' those
gathered 'round this table...

*The entire household, nuns included, are standing around the
dining room table, its surface groaning with food. Although his
head is bowed, Michael glances across the table at Daphne, who
is stealing similar glances at him and smiling as well. Fiona, of
course, observes this wordless tennis exchange between her two
favorite people and smiles.*

SISTER JOSEPHINE
...we humbly offer up our
prayers o' Thanksgivin' in this
year of His Lord, eighteen
hundred 'n' ninety-seven.
Though it be a new holiday for
those of us from the ol' sod,
tis with an open heart we be
embracin' our new country's
ways 'n' traditions. 'N' for the
bounty o' feast 'n' good
harvest laid before us...

*SFX: A little gasp of pain from Catherine.*

*A few of the bowed heads look down the table at her. She
offers an apologetic, grimaced smile, one hand on her very large
mid-section.*

SISTER JOSEPHINE (CONT'D)
...may we all be rememberin'
those less fortunate whose
plates are empty o' food 'n'

whose chairs are empty as well
o' those who--

*SFX: A louder groan from Catherine.*

*Aghast, she looks down at the floor, as does Ian. Total silence
has fallen on the entire table. No one knows quite what to do.
Determined to finish the rest of her Thanksgiving grace,
however, Sister Josephine opens her mouth to continue.*

SISTER JOSEPHINE (CONT'D)
We ask y, Lord, that--

DAPHNE
Bloody hell! Do you all have
the sense of a *radish*?! This
woman is having a *baby*!

*The group is even more petrified.*

DAPHNE
*Do* something!

*MONTAGE*

*In the flicker-speed fashion of a Keystone Cops scene, everyone
bursts from the dining table at once to start fetching water,
fetching towels, getting Catherine upstairs, pacing in anxiety
and colliding with each other. The warp-drive montage ends
with Sister Bridget closing the bedroom door.*

INT. CORRIDOR - CONTINUOUS

*Ian is pacing back and forth, Michael is smoking a pipe, and
the nuns are praying.*

IAN
(to Michael)
How long has it been?

MICHAEL
(checks pocketwatch)
Five minutes since the last
time y' asked.

*SFX: The wail of a baby crying.*

*Ian grins and goes to give Michael a hug. The nuns grin, too,
and cross themselves.*

*The door opens and Fiona and Daphne emerge, the latter
carrying the newborn baby. Daphne places the child in Ian's
arms.*

DAPHNE
Congratulations, Mr.
Sutherland. You've got
yourself a son.

*The nuns all draw close to take an admiring look at the
household's new addition.*

FIONA
(to Ian)
She's been askin' for y', if y'
want to go in.

*Ian, flummoxed about what to do with the new baby, hastily
hands him to Michael and rushes in to see how his wife is
doing. Fiona follows him in. Michael, on unfamiliar ground,
is nevertheless honored to be holding a new life in his hands.
He looks up and sees Daphne smiling at him.*

MICHAEL
(off baby)
I wouldn't mind havin' one o'
these myself someday.

DAPHNE
Then perhaps you should
think of getting yourself a
wife.

*She coquettishly winks at him and goes in to see how the new mother is doing.*

INT. BEDROOM - CONTINUOUS

*An exhausted Catherine is lying in bed; Sister Honore is holding her hand. Catherine reaches out her free hand to Ian as he approaches.*

CATHERINE
I couldn't have done it without
them.

IAN
Aye. Neither could the rest of
us.

*CU of champagne glasses--and one teacup--being clinked.*

INT. DINING ROOM - LATER

*Michael, Ian, Daphne and Fiona toast the new arrival.*

IAN
To Ian Michael Joseph
Seamus William Robert

Gilbert Birdie Malcolm Angus
Sutherland!

MICHAEL
'N' what will y' be callin' him
for short?

*They all laugh.*


INT. BOARD ROOM - DAY

*In contrast, the tobacco executives sit around the table in stony
silence.*

PIERPONT
They shouldn't be doing this
well.

BLOUNT
They shouldn't but they are.

GRIGGS
It's the nuns. They're doing
something.

PIERPONT
Doing what?

GRIGGS
I don't know. But they must
be doing <u>something</u>.

PIERPONT
How are the plans coming for
adding workers to our own
plantations?

BLOUNT
Not well.

GRIGGS
Not a single convent on the
entire Eastern Seaboard wants
to come work for us for free.

PIERPONT
Hmmm...

GRIGGS
What about immigrants?

BLOUNT
*They'll* work for a lower wage.

GRIGGS
And be happy to have a job.

PIERPONT
That's quite possibly the
stupidest idea I've ever heard.

*Griggs and Blount sink lower in their seats.*

PIERPONT (CONT'D)
What are you going to say
next? That we should send all
of our tobacco plants across
the oceans of the world so
they don't have to leave home
at all?!

GRIGGS
(meekly)
It was just a thought.

PIERPONT
Well think of something *better*!
We can't let another year roll
by without acquiring that land!


I/E. PLANTATION - DAY

*MONTAGE*

*The household is getting ready for Christmas. The nuns are decorating, Deliah is preparing sumptuous holiday treats, Sister Honore and Sister Bridget are playing with Catherine and Ian's baby.*


INT. PARLOR - CONTINUOUS

*Daphne is standing on a step-stool as she decorates the massive tree. As she goes to hang an ornament, she loses her balance. To her surprise--and relief--she falls into Michael's arms.*

MICHAEL
Not to worry, lass. I'll always
be here to catch y' if y' fall.

*As he sets her safely on the ground, the sensual sparks fly between them, compelling the nearest nuns to giggle in amusement. Fiona, observing all of this, looks heavenward.*

FIONA
(in a whisper)
I'd not be mindin', y' know, if
y' could move 'em along a wee
bit faster...


INT. PARLOR - EVENING

*CU of a spoon being clinked against a crystal glass by Michael.*

*A houseful of Christmas GUESTS, plus the nuns, have turned out to celebrate the season. Their chatter dies down as they turn their attention to Michael. Fiona proudly stands next to him.*

MICHAEL
My darlin' sister Fiona tells me
we've a special treat in store
this evenin'.

FIONA
The Sisters o' Thistle have
been practicin' a few songs o'
the season 'n' wish to be
singin' 'em for y'.

*The crowd claps appreciatively as the nuns with their songbooks, minus Sister Honore and Sister Bridget, take their place around the piano which will be played by Sister Josephine.*

*Sister Josephine plays the first few bars of SILENT NIGHT. The nuns open their mouths to sing...and it is absolutely awful. Though zealous in spirit and enthusiasm, music is clearly not their forte. The guests try to maintain cringing smiles of enjoyment. Even Fiona looks dismayed that this is not quite coming across as she had hoped.*

*Sister Honore moves through the crowd to whisper something to her. Fiona looks over at Daphne, who is standing next to Michael and looking breathtakingly beautiful. She then tiptoes over to Sister Josephine and whispers in her ear. Sister Josephine proceeds to play faster which, in turn, compels the nuns to sing faster to keep up.*

*When they finish, the guests applaud, largely because they are relieved that their torture is over. The nuns start to turn to the next page of their songbooks.*

FIONA
(to guests)
I've just been informed we've
had a special request for a
solo.

*The nuns, standing behind her, look confused by this announcement.*

FIONA
If I could be askin' Miss
Daphne Hedges to step
forward?

*Puzzled, Daphne leaves Michael's side.*

FIONA (CONT'D)
Miss Hedges will be singin' the
Christmas favorite, *O Holy
Night.*
(under her breath to
Daphne)
Y' *do* know the words to it,
don't y'?

*The guests are applauding, leaving Daphne little choice but to reluctantly comply. She nods, and Sister Josephine flips to the right page of music.*

*Sister Josephine proceeds to play. Daphne opens her mouth to sing and it is the voice of an angel, mesmerizing everyone in the room, not the least of whom is Sister Honore. When she finishes the song, in fact, it is Sister Honore who starts clapping first and nods her approval to Daphne.*

*Daphne returns to her place next to Michael, who is absolutely awestruck. He takes her hand and, oblivious to the guests and the commotion around them, declares his feelings.*

MICHAEL
From the first day I laid eyes
on y' at the harbor, Daphne, I
knew my life had changed
forever.

DAPHNE
And how, exactly, do you
mean to act on that?

MICHAEL
By tellin' y that if the entire
world were to change
tomorrow, I'd ne'er be happier
than I am at this very moment.

*He leans in to kiss her for the first time.*

*SFX: Explosion*

*CU of various national newspaper headlines that The Maine
has been attacked, triggering the start of the Spanish American
War.*

INT. DINING ROOM - MORNING

*Fiona enters for breakfast to find a glum Ian and Michael
looking at the newspapers.*

FIONA
(candidly)
If your chins were any longer,
they'd be hittin' the floor.

*The two men exchange a look with one another.*

MICHAEL
(with difficulty)
Ian 'n' myself are goin' to war.

FIONA
(as she pours herself
tea)
'N' what's it about this time?

IAN
We'll be leavin' to fight the
Spanish.

FIONA
The Spanish, is it? 'N' what did
Spain ever do to Scotland?

MICHAEL
It's what she did to the US of
A that's got us hoppin' mad.

IAN
(points to headline)
Remember the Maine!

FIONA
The main what?

*Michael takes Fiona's tea cup from her and sets it down in
order to take both of her hands.*

MICHAEL
I made a promise I'd ne'er be
leavin' y' again.

FIONA
Aye.

MICHAEL
Tis a promise I'll need to
break.

FIONA
Michael--

MICHAEL
Only a little 'n' not for very
long.

*Fiona looks from one to the other.*

FIONA
Will y' be in danger?

MICHAEL
Sure as there'd be <u>more</u> in
danger than ourselves if we let
the likes o' Spain get away with
bloody murder.

FIONA
What about Daphne...and
Catherine?

MICHAEL
I'll be makin' provisions.
Power of attorney, it's called.
Should Ian or myself not be
findin' our way back--

*She quickly puts her hand to his lips.*

FIONA
Don't even say it.  Don't.


EXT. PLANTATION - DUSK

*Daphne has not taken Michael's announcement very well.*

DAPHNE
You're a farmer, Michael
McKay, not a fighter!  Not to
mention, it's not even *your*
fight you're running off to!

MICHAEL
Tis America's fight 'n' that
makes it mine as well.

DAPHNE
For how long?

MICHAEL
Til it's over.

DAPHNE
And how long is that?

MICHAEL
No more than a few weeks, I'd
think.

DAPHNE
(snort)
That's what they said about
the War of the Roses...

MICHAEL
I didn't come to mix words
with y', Daphne.  I came to
ask y' to wait for me.

DAPHNE
And what about the <u>next</u> one?
And the one after? Will you
drop everything you care

about to go fight those as
well?

MICHAEL
Sure as there won't <u>be</u> a next
one when they see what
Americans can do! All I'm
askin', lass, is that y' give me a
reason to come back.

*A painfully long moment of silence hangs between them.*

DAPHNE
I'll think about it.


INT. DINING ROOM - LATER

*CU of Fiona signing legal papers.*

*She hands them across the table to Catherine to sign, too. This
act is witnessed by Michael and Ian's attorney, WILLIAM
MARBLES, a bespectacled young man who is very nice but
not exactly a force to be reckoned with.)*

WILLIAM
(taking papers from
Catherine)
That should take care of
anything that arises.

*Fiona, with tears in her eyes, looks anxiously at Michael, who
closes his hand over hers.*

MICHAEL
Not to worry yourself.
William here is as good a
solicitor as they come.

FIONA
I'd be feelin' better if you 'n'
Ian were stayin'.

MICHAEL
Hush y' now. We'll be back
before the ink dries. I
promise.

FIONA
Might I be remindin' y' that
your last promise took 16
years!

*SFX: Thunder and rain*

EXT. VERANDA - RAINY MORNING

*Ian is saying goodbye to Catherine and his son. The servants
and nuns have assembled to see the two men off; the nuns are
crossing themselves. Michael looks at his pocketwatch.
Daphne is nowhere in sight.*

FIONA
I'll tell her y' said goodbye.

MICHAEL
Will y' promise me somethin'
else as well?

FIONA
If I can.

*He leans in and whispers something to her. Fiona considers his
words a moment.*

FIONA (CONT'D)
If it be the Lord's wish for y'
to be together, y' needn't
worry about her wanderin' off.

*With reluctance, he goes to join Ian in the waiting carriage. As it starts to roll away, Daphne suddenly pushes her way through the nuns and runs down the steps after it.*

DAPHNE
Michael!

*The carriage lurches to a sudden stop. Michael steps out. Oblivious to the rain, they meet in a passionate embrace and a soul-drenching kiss that is the stuff of movie magic. The nuns applaud their approval.*

*SFX: Lesser applause and the clink of champagne glasses.*

INT. BOARD ROOM - DAY

*Pierpont is leading his cohorts in a toast.*

PIERPONT
By engaging us in war,
gentlemen, the Spanish have
just done us an enormous
favor. We may have lost one
of our valiant ships but, in the
end, we're about to gain some
of the finest land in Virginia.

ALL
Here, here!

*SFX: Knock on door*

## EXT. ESTATE FRONT DOOR - MORNING

*Sister Josephine opens the front door to reveal Blount and Griggs, who politely tip their hats.*

BLOUNT
A pleasant good morning, uh--
Sister. I'm Lionel Blount.

GRIGGS
And Harry Griggs.

SISTER JOSEPHINE
(puzzled)
Aye.

GRIGGS
(checks pocketwatch)
Our apology for being late.
We're here to see Mr. McKay.

SISTER JOSEPHINE
Y' be late all right. Mr. McKay
is off fightin' the Spanish.

BLOUNT
(feigning
astonishment)
Is he now?
(looks to Griggs)

GRIGGS
We don't have the wrong day,
do we?

BLOUNT
(to Sister Josephine)
It is Tuesday, isn't it?

SISTER JOSEPHINE
Aye.

GRIGGS
Perhaps Mr. Sutherland then.
Is *he* in?

SISTER JOSEPHINE
Mr. Sutherland is with Mr.
McKay.

BLOUNT
Well, this *is* confusing, isn't it?
Perhaps we could speak with
whomever is in charge...?

*Sister Josephine thinks on this a moment and closes the door.*
*A moment later, it is opened by Fiona.*

FIONA
Might I be helpin' y'
gentlemen?

BLOUNT
And you are?

FIONA
Fiona McKay.  Michael
McKay's sister.

GRIGGS
Well, Miss--er, Sister McKay,
I'm sure you can clear this up.
(hands her some
papers)
We spoke to your brother
about his selling this property.
I'm sure you'll find everything
in order.

FIONA
Surely y' must be mistaken.
My brother said no such thing.

BLOUNT
Yes, well, probably in the
excitement of going off to
war--

GRIGGS
Remember the Maine!

BLOUNT
--he must have forgotten.

GRIGGS
(off papers)
You'll find everything in order.

FIONA
(hands them back)
We've no intention of sellin' at all.

BLOUNT
But certainly the price--

*Fiona firmly closes the door.*


INT. BOARD ROOM - LATER

PIERPONT
(annoyed)
And that was it?

GRIGGS
She didn't even invite us in.

PIERPONT
They're *nuns*, for Christ's sake!
This shouldn't be that difficult.

BLOUNT
She said they wouldn't sell.

PIERPONT
He put her up to it. I'm sure of it.

GRIGGS
So what do we do now?

PIERPONT
What I do is go back. And
make them an offer they can't
refuse.

*CU: Knock on front door*


EXT. ESTATE FRONT DOOR - MORNING

*This time the door is opened by Catherine.*

CATHERINE
May I help you?

PIERPONT
(pleasantly surprised)
And to whom do I have the
pleasure of addressing this
glorious Virginia morning?

CATHERINE
I'm Mrs. Catherine Sutherland.

PIERPONT
(gasp)
*Ian's* bride?
(kisses her hand)
Then I'm doubly charmed.

CATHERINE
(on guard)
And *your* name, sir?

PIERPONT
Cornelius Pierpont.  One of many
admirers of your husband.  I
understand he and his partner Mr.
McKay are off fighting those
wicked Spanish?

CATHERINE
We expect their return any
day.

PIERPONT
(withdraws paperwork)
Well I'm sure this will sweeten
their homecoming
immeasurably.

CATHERINE
(looks at it)
There seems to be a mistake.

PIERPONT
The only mistake, dear lady, is that
you were not born a twin so that I
might engage your company at
supper...


INT. DINING ROOM - EVENING

*Fiona and Catherine have invited William to dinner. He looks over the papers Pierpont has dropped off.*

WILLIAM
(incredulous)
If I hadn't seen it for myself--

FIONA
Does he mean to be cheatin' us
then?

WILLIAM
Oh it's *more* than fair market
value, Fiona.  Given what the
lands around here have been
going for--

CATHERINE
Why does he want *this* land?

WILLIAM
Because of the soil.
(shrug)
I don't know.  It's almost as if
it has some sort of divine
blessing for growing the best
tobacco.

FIONA
But sure as they've got crops
enough o' their own...?

WILLIAM
For greedy men, that's never
enough.  Until they get you to
agree to sell, they're not going
to back down.

CATHERINE
So what you're saying, then, is that
we've got a fight on our hands?

FIONA
'N a fight they're intendin' to win?

*He opens his mouth to speak but he's pre-empted by Daphne,
standing in the doorway.*

DAPHNE
Only until they play their last card.
(a cryptic beat)
And that's when *we* win.


EXT. KING STREET - DAY

*A black carriage drawn by black horses pulls up in front of the
building housing the tobacco company's upstairs office. A
FOOTMAN immediately alights to open the carriage door.
We see a pair of expensive black boots and the hem of a black
cape. A massive MAN ("JH") with silver hair whom we only
see from the back strides toward the doors with a commanding,
purposeful gait reminiscent of Darth Vader. In fact, if you
were to combine Darth Vader with Orson Welles, this is
probably the guy you would get. Two DOORMEN open the
front doors for him.*


INT. BOARD ROOM - CONTINUOUS

*Pierpont, Blount, Griggs, et al are contemplating their current
dilemma, unaware that their problems are about to worsen
significantly.*

BLOUNT
The usual smear tactics won't
work.

GRIGGS
Everyone loves them.

PIERPONT
(with a snarl)
So I've heard.

BLOUNT
(suddenly inspired)
What if we were to spread the
rumor that they're actually
witches only *pretending* to be
nuns?

*There are bobble-heads of consensus around the table that this
is an intriguing idea.*

GRIGGS
(excitedly joins in)
And that we want to protect
innocent children from their
clutches by warning them of
the dangers of prolonged
exposure.

PIERPONT
Hmm.


EXT. DOUBLE DOORS OUTSIDE
BOARDROOM

*POV of "JH" striding toward entrance to board room. A
pair of startled UPSTAIRS DOORMEN rush to fling open
the doors.*


INT. BOARD ROOM - CONTINUOUS

*Everyone except Pierpont, whose back is to the doors, bolt from their chairs and spring to attention at the unexpected and intimidating sight of their chairman. Pierpont looks around and scrambles to his feet as well.*

PIERPONT
(clearly discomfited)
Mr. Chairman! Uh--what a
surprise.

*With a shrug of his broad shoulders, JH drops his cape, which is dutifully grabbed up by one of the doormen.*

PIERPONT (CONT'D)
We had no idea you were
coming, sir. Did you have a
pleasant--

*JH interrupts, fixing him in a steely glare.*

JH
(his accent is British)
It would appear that quite a <u>lot</u>
of things have been slipping
through your fingers lately.
My new planation, for
instance.

*Pierpont starts to sit back down and feign control.*

PIERPONT
Yes sir, as a matter of fact, we
were just--

JH
Get out of my chair.

*Pierpont instantly complies. The others, too terrified to move, wait until JH takes his place at the head of the table before*

113

*cautiously returning to their seats. Pierpont, of course, is now chairless and growing squirmy.*

JH (CONT'D)
I understand the papers have
yet to be signed.  Is that true?

PIERPONT
We're working on it even as we
speak.

JH
I didn't sail clear across the
Atlantic to hear that you're
"working on it", Pierpont.

PIERPONT
No, sir.

JH
It should have been done months ago.

PIERPONT
Yes, sir, but--

JH
How do you account for that?

PIERPONT
We've--uh--encountered a few
obstacles in the acquisition
process.

JH
What sort of obstacles?

PIERPONT
(beat)
Nuns.

JH
Excuse me?

PIERPONT
Nuns.

JH
Nuns?

*JH looks to the rest of the board.*

JH (CONT'D)
Am I to understand,
gentlemen, that *nuns* are
standing in the way of this
company's progress?

BLOUNT
(attempting a lame
save)
We *have* heard a rumor that
they might also be witches...

*Pierpont shoots Blount a "shut-up-you're-not-helping-here"*
*look.*

JH
(to Pierpont)
What about the offer that I
authorized?

PIERPONT
They refused it.

JH
And the second offer?

PIERPONT
They-uh--refused that as well.

JH
What are they holding out for?

PIERPONT
We--uh--don't really know
how nuns think these things
through.  But let me assure
you, JH, that--

JH
Pierpont?

PIERPONT
Yes?

JH
Shut up.

PIERPONT
Yes, sir.

JH
Obviously I shall have to take
matters into my own hands.

*He stands, prompting everyone else to stand as well.*

JH (CONT'D)
If I were you, gentlemen, I
would not anticipate receipt of
a Christmas bonus this year.

ALL
(solemnly, in unison)
Yes, Mr. Chairman.

*One of the doormen is already standing at the ready with his cape.*

JH
(icily)
I shall pay a visit to these
"nuns" tomorrow morning.

*He starts to leave. Pierpont makes one last effort to grovel.*

PIERPONT
Will there be anything else, sir?

*With glacial slowness, JH turns to look at him.*

JH
Yes, as a matter of fact, there
*is* one more thing.
(beat)
You're fired.


EXT. STARRY NIGHT SKY

FIONA (O.C.)
I know it's not your way to be
handin' us more troubles than
we know what to do with.


INT. FIONA'S ROOM - EVENING

*Fiona is on her knees in prayer at the open window.*

FIONA
Nor to be desertin' us when
the times get hard. Tis your
way o' makin' us stronger 'n'
more faithful 'n' trustin' there's
all a grand plan to it.
(beat)

But lately, Lord, I've been
askin' myself 'n' wonderin'
what exactly y' have in mind
'n' why y' made Michael put
me in charge.

SISTER HONORE (O.C.)
Because He knows you have
an honest heart.

*Walking slowly and with the aid of a cane, the elderly nun
comes to the window to join her.*

FIONA
I didn't hear y' come in.

SISTER HONORE
(wisely)
Just as y' sometimes think He
doesn't hear so well either?

FIONA
(embarrassed)
What y' heard me say to Him
just now--

SISTER HONORE
Sure as we all question it
sometimes, Fiona.  Myself
bein' no exception.

*Fiona tilts her head in surprise at this revelation.*

SISTER HONORE (CONT'D)
Aye.

*The two women gaze out at the stars for a long moment.*

FIONA
How do y' know when y' do
the right thing? The tobacco
men, I mean. What if we're
makin' a mistake by sayin' no?

SISTER HONORE
You'll not be knowin' that,
lass, til y' see how it all washes
out.

FIONA
(deep sigh)
I was afraid y'd say that.

*She notices the Mother Superior's troubled look as she returns
her gaze to the stars.*

FIONA (CONT'D)
Was there somethin' else on
your mind?

*Sister Honore hesitates.*

SISTER HONORE
(gravely)
There's somethin' y' need to
know...about Daphne.

FIONA
What's to know? She's my
dearest friend.
(confidentially)
'N when Michael comes home,
she's to be my sister as well.

SISTER HONORE
Aye. 'N that's why y' both
need to know she's got a past.

FIONA
Y' mean about her runnin'
away?

SISTER HONORE
So y' knew about that?

FIONA
(in suspicion)
How did *you* know about that?

SISTER HONORE
A week or so before we left
Scotland, a man came lookin'
for her at the abbey. He told
us who he was 'n' said he'd not
be leavin' without her.

FIONA
(alarmed)
Y' didn't tell him where she'd gone?

SISTER HONORE
He loves her, Fiona. He wants
her back.

FIONA
But y' didn't tell him?

SISTER HONORE
How could I be tellin' what I
didn't know? Since y' never
made mention of her after y'
left--

FIONA
Only because I knew she
wasn't a favorite--

SISTER HONORE
He'll not stop lookin' til he
finds her, y' know. 'N when he
does--

FIONA
If he does.

SISTER HONORE
Goin' back would be the right
thing.  Y' need to tell her that.

FIONA
Not if she means to be happy.

SISTER HONORE
He seemed a force y'd not
want to trifle with.

FIONA
Aye.  But neither is she.

CUT TO:

*CU of Michael's hand as he writes a letter by candlelight.*

MICHAEL (V.O.)
Dearest Fiona.  The man I
wrote y' about--Colonel
Roosevelt?--he says we're all to
be comin' home soon.  Ian 'n'
myself are countin' the days to
be sure.  Will be keepin' this
short but wanted to inquire if
y'd had any troubles.  Sure as
you've got a good head on
your shoulders 'n' Catie, too.  I
can't imagine any problem the

both o' y' couldn't handle.  All
my love, Michael.  P.S. My
love to Daphne as well.  Keep
askin' her to wait for me.

EXT. PLANTATION - MORNING

*The black carriage drawn by the black horses is approaching
the house.  It stops and, as before, we see the same black boots
and black cape.*

EXT. FRONT DOOR

*POV of JH's hand knocking on the door.*

INT. FOYER - CONTINUOUS

*A NUN with a basket of laundry starts toward the door to
answer it.  Daphne, who is passing through, waves her away.*

DAPHNE
Go on with what you're doing.
I'll get it.

*She opens the door.  JH does a double-take when he sees her.
As does she.*

JH
Daphne?

DAPHNE
Father?

JH
What the bloody hell are *you*
doing here?

DAPHNE
What the bloody hell are *you*
doing here?


INT. JUST OUTSIDE THE CLOSED DINING
ROOM DOORS - MOMENTS LATER

*SFX: Muffled shouting, the crash of a vase*

*A gaggle of nuns are straining to hear what's going on. Fiona,
walking past, stops in curiosity.*

FIONA
What are y' doin'?

*The nuns turn to "shush" her. She draws closer.*

FIONA (CONT'D)
(repeats in a whisper)
What are y' doin'?

*An ELDERLY NUN whispers reply.*

ELDERLY NUN
Daphne 'n' her father are
havin' a row.

CUT TO:


INT. SISTER HONORE'S ROOM

FIONA
Her father?!

SISTER HONORE
Aye. The man who came
askin' for her at Thistleburn.

FIONA
(confused)
But sure as I thought y' were
talkin' about the hippo in the
waistcoat!

SISTER HONORE
Your words are a puzzle,
Fiona.

FIONA
The man she was betrothed
to.  Isn't *he* the one y' said was
wantin' her back?

SISTER HONORE
Well I wouldn't be knowin' a
thing about that.  I only know
her Da was beside himself in
not knowin' if she be alive or
dead.


INT. DINING ROOM - CONTINUOUS

DAPHNE
You've never cared if I was
alive or dead!  All you've ever
cared about are your bloody
profits!

JH
That's not true, Daphne.  I've
cared about your happiness a
great deal.

DAPHNE
By trying to marry me off to a
man I didn't love?

JH
(matter of factly)
I didn't love your mother when we
married...but, over time, I came to.

DAPHNE
Well I don't love Horace, I
never will, and I'm not going
back!


INT. JUST OUTSIDE THE CLOSED DINING
ROOM DOORS

*Catherine is now walking past and is curious about what
everyone is straining to hear through the doors.*

CATHERINE
What's going on?

*The nuns "shush" her. She goes up to Fiona, who is also
intently listening.*

CATHERINE (CONT'D)
(whispered)
What's going on?

FIONA
It's Daphne. She's not
marryin' Horace.

CATHERINE
Who's Horace?


INT. DINING ROOM - CONTINUOUS

JH
You're as difficult as your late
mother.

DAPHNE
Then why should my demands
surprise you?

JH
(sputtering)
Because they're unreasonable!

DAPHNE
You're only saying that
because they're not in accord
with yours.

JH
The only thing standing
between you and the perfectly
respectable life I had planned
for you from the day you were
first born is your damned
English stubbornness!

DAPHNE
(sly smile)
And the only thing standing
between you and what you
*really* came here to get...is me.

INT. JUST OUTSIDE THE CLOSED DINING
ROOM DOORS

*Daphne unexpectedly opens the doors, making it difficult for
everyone who was eavesdropping to pretend otherwise. She steps
into their midst with the self-satisfied look of someone in total
control.*

DAPHNE (CONT'D)
Ladies...I believe we've
reached consensus.


INT. BOARD ROOM - DAY

*JH, William, Fiona, Daphne and Catherine are seated at the
end of the table; JH's associates are in attendance as well and
witnessing the signing of the papers. William hands Catherine
a document.*

WILLIAM
You're the expert on numbers.
Does the new offer and 20%
profit share meet with your
approval?

*Catherine looks at it, hands it to Fiona with a nod.*

CATHERINE
It's more than generous.
Especially if smoking
continues to catch on.

JH
(grumbling)
Damned thievery if you ask
me!
(to William)
For what I'm paying, it should
include the house as well!

*Fiona tilts her head toward the other end of the table.*

FIONA
'N would y' mean to be puttin'
em all out on the street?

*We see that all the good sisters are seated and witnessing this momentous transaction. JH is visibly discomfited to have them staring at him in earnest.*

FIONA (O.C.)
Sure as y'd not want it on your
conscience to do such a thing.

WILLIAM
(off documents)
Per Article 6, Clause 17 of the
agreement, title to the house
shall not revert to corporate
ownership until the last Sister
of the Order of Thistle has
entered the Kingdom of
Heaven.

*The nuns are happy campers and nod among themselves that this clause in the contract is a very good thing.*

JH
Whatever. Are we finished
yet?

*Daphne clears her throat. Everyone looks at her.*

DAPHNE
Aren't you forgetting
something, Father dear?

*All eyes are now upon JH.*

JH
Fine. I hereby give my
blessing and consent for my
daughter to stay in America
and marry whomever she
damn well pleases.

*Everyone applauds.*

*Applause dissolves into the sound of carriage wheels turning.*

TITLE CARD: TWO MONTHS LATER


EXT. PLANTATION - DAY

*A carriage is turning onto the grounds of the plantation.*


INT. CARRIAGE - CONTINUOUS

*Michael and Ian are returning home.*

IAN
(looks out window)
Holy Mother o' God but there
be a sight for sore eyes!

*Michael looks out as well on the workers amongst the crops.*

MICHAEL
Aye, it is.

*As Ian continues talking, Michael starts to lean back, then
scowls and looks out the window again.*

IAN
'N what stories we'll have to
be tellin'! Especially about
that Colonel Roosevelt.
Bigger than life he was,
wouldn't y' say? 'N what was
that funny word he was always
usin' when he'd lead a charge?

MICHAEL
Ian?

IAN
Aye?

MICHAEL
(off workers)
Do any of 'em look familiar?

*Ian leans forward and looks.*

IAN
Can't say as they do. Maybe it's
just 'cause we've been gone so
long.

*Camera slowly pulls out for CRANE-SHOT, revealing that
the plantation now has hundreds of workers as opposed to the
handful the first time we saw it.*

MICHAEL (O.S.)
Seems to me as there's *more* of
'em as well, do y' think?

IAN (O.S.)
Perhaps they hired an extra
hand or two to fill in.


EXT. VERANDA

*Catherine and Fiona are chatting with some nuns on the
veranda. Catherine sees the carriage first and, with a cry of
delight, hands the baby off to Fiona and runs down the steps
and out to greet it. Not wanting to be left out, Fiona hands off
the baby to one of the sisters and follows her.*

*Ian alights first and runs to scoop up Catherine in his arms.
Fiona runs up to meet Michael.*

FIONA
(laughs and hugs him)
It's about time the winds blew
y' back!

MICHAEL
Did y' miss me then?

FIONA
Aye but we did!  'N are y'
home to stay permanent?

MICHAEL
If the Lord be willin'.  So tell
me about the land.

FIONA
The land?

MICHAEL
Did y' have any trouble?

*Fiona starts to reply but is pre-empted by Daphne.*

DAPHNE (O.C.)
Michael!

*Michael breaks into a wide grin when he sees her. Forgetting
his question to Fiona, he breaks into a run to meet her. Fiona
fondly watches their reunion.*

FIONA
Nothin' we couldn't handle.
(glances heavenward)
With a little help along the way...


FADE TO BLACK

## ABOUT THE AUTHOR

Former actress and director Christina Hamlett is an award-winning author whose credits to date include 35 books, 163 stage plays, 5 optioned feature films, and squillions of articles and interviews that appear online and in trade publications throughout the world. She is also a script consultant for stage and screen as well as a professional ghostwriter.
Learn more at www.authorhamlett.com

Made in the USA
Columbia, SC
20 September 2021